TECUMSEH

BY WALTER LAPLANTE

 Gareth Stevens
PUBLISHING

Please visit our website, www.garethstevens.com. For a free color catalog of all our high-quality books, call toll free 1-800-542-2595 or fax 1-877-542-2596.

Library of Congress Cataloging-in-Publication Data

LaPlante, Walter.
  Tecumseh / Walter LaPlante.
      pages cm. — (Native American heroes)
  Includes bibliographical references and index.
  ISBN 978-1-4824-2704-2 (pbk.)
  ISBN 978-1-4824-2705-9 (6 pack)
  ISBN 978-1-4824-2706-6 (library binding)
  1. Tecumseh, Shawnee chief, 1768-1813—Juvenile literature. 2. Shawnee Indians—Biography—Juvenile literature. I. Title.
  E99.S35L38 2015
  977.004973170092—dc23
  [B]
                                        2015009818

Published in 2016 by
Gareth Stevens Publishing
111 East 14th Street, Suite 349
New York, NY 10003

Copyright © 2016 Gareth Stevens Publishing

Designer: Laura Bowen
Editor: Kristen Rajczak

Photo credits: Cover, pp. 1, 13, 19 MPI/Archive Photos/Getty Images; cover, pp. 1–24 (series art) Binkski/Shutterstock.com; p. 5 Culture Club/Hulton Archive/Getty Images; p. 7 blinkblink/Shutterstock.com; p. 9 De Agostini Picture Library/De Agostini/Getty Images; p. 11 Kean Collection/Archive Photos/Getty Images; p. 15 Universal Images Group/Getty Images; p. 17 Universal History Archive/Universal Images Group/Getty Images; p. 21 Rosser1954/Wikimedia Commons.

Printed in the United States of America

CPSIA compliance information: Batch #CS15GS: For further information contact Gareth Stevens, New York, New York at 1-800-542-2595.

CONTENTS

Boldface words appear in the glossary.

Taking a Stand

During the late 1700s and early 1800s, Native Americans had someone speaking up for their rights. His name was Tecumseh. Tecumseh was a brave fighter and a great **orator**. He worked hard to **preserve** Native American ways of life.

5

Family Life

Tecumseh was born around 1768 in present-day Ohio. He grew up around his father's **tribe**, the Shawnee. Because Tecumseh's father died and his mother went to live in Missouri, Tecumseh was raised by his sister and a Shawnee chief named Blackfish.

Lake Huron

Lake Ontario

New York

Michigan

Lake Michigan

Lake Erie

Pennsylvania

Ohio

historical Shawnee homelands

Maryland

Indiana

West Virginia

Virginia

Kentucky

UNITED STATES

North Carolina

Tennessee

South Carolina

7

Fighting with Words

White settlers began taking over Native American land, angering many Native Americans, including Tecumseh. But during **raids** against the settlers, Tecumseh saw the Shawnee treat them **cruelly**. Tecumseh spoke against this terrible **treatment**. He learned his words could have power.

Tecumseh became known among the Shawnee for his bravery in battle. By 1800, he was **representing** Native Americans in talks with the US government. Many people respected Tecumseh for his skill as an orator and leader of his people.

In 1808, Tecumseh and his brother founded Prophetstown. They opposed the US government taking more of their homelands. Tecumseh traveled around the country speaking to other tribes about the problem. He wanted them to work together.

Battle of Tippecanoe

In 1810, Tecumseh met General William Henry Harrison, and the two nearly fought. While Tecumseh was away in 1811, his brother led the Shawnee against Harrison's forces near Prophetstown. The town was destroyed in what's now called the Battle of Tippecanoe.

15

At War

In 1812, a war between Great Britain and the United States began. Tecumseh stopped his efforts to bring Native Americans together and decided to join the fight. He traveled to Canada with his followers to side with the British.

17

Tecumseh played an important part in the British taking Detroit. But, not long after, US soldiers led by General Harrison pushed the British back into Canada. During the Battle of the Thames in October 1813, Tecumseh died.

19

Honored in Death

No one knows who killed Tecumseh or where his body is buried. But his story remains one of the great tales of a Native American hero. Today, ships, towns, and schools have all been named after the brave Shawnee leader Tecumseh.

THE LIFE OF TECUMSEH

around 1768
Tecumseh is born in Ohio.

1808
Tecumseh founds Prophetstown with his brother.

1810
Tecumseh meets General William Henry Harrison.

1811
The Shawnee lose the Battle of Tippecanoe.

1812
The War of 1812 begins.

1813
Tecumseh dies during the Battle of the Thames.

GLOSSARY

cruelly: having to do with causing pain and not feeling sorry about it

orator: one who gives speeches, especially in a formal setting

preserve: to keep something in its original state

raid: a sudden attack

represent: to stand for

treatment: the way someone thinks or acts toward someone or something

tribe: a group of people who live, work, and move about together

FOR MORE INFORMATION

BOOKS

McGovern, Ann. *Native American Heroes: Osceola, Tecumseh & Cochise.* New York, NY: Scholastic, 2013.

Zimmerman, Dwight Jon. *Tecumseh: Shooting Star of the Shawnee.* New York, NY: Sterling, 2010.

WEBSITES

Native American Facts for Kids: Shawnee Tribe
www.bigorrin.org/shawnee_kids.htm
Read more about Tecumseh's people, the Shawnee.

Native Americans: Tecumseh
www.ducksters.com/history/native_americans/tecumseh.php
Learn all about Tecumseh, and find links to websites about other Native American heroes.

INDEX